WHALES
of the World

by June Behrens

CHILDRENS PRESS ®

CHICAGO

PHOTO CREDITS

© Camerique/H. Armstrong Roberts—48

Bruce Coleman:
  © J & D Bartlett—5, 21, 38
  © Jeff Foott—11 (left), 24
  © Keith Gunnar—30 (left)
  © Norman Myers—32
  © G. Williamson—11 (right)

Earthviews:
  © Ken Balcomb—39
  © Larry Foster—20, 28
  © Gregory Silber—22, 29 (2 photos)
  © Ted Stephensen—34 (right)
  © G.R. Williamson—26
  © J. Michael Williamson—12

Marilyn Gartman Agency:
  © Arnold H. Crane—40
  © Ellis Herwig—3

© Photri—44

© Eda Rogers—31

Tom Stack & Associates:
  © Jeff Foott—10, 25, back cover
  © Brian Parker—41
  © Ed Robinson—4, 9
  © Tom Stack—33
  © Jack D. Swenson—37

© Lynn Stone—8 (right)
© Bernie Tershy—19
© Tershey & Strong—27

Valan Photos:
  © Michel Bourque—8 (left), 23, 35
  © Kennon Cooke—1
  © A. Farquhar—15
  © S. Krasemann—30 (right), back cover
  © Dannis W. Schmidt—14
  © Richard Sears—6, 7, 13, 16, 17, 18, 34 (left),
    36, 42, 45, front cover

© Karen Yops—43

Cover: Tail of a blue whale
Back cover: Gray whale off Vancouver Island
            Bottlenose dolphins
Title page: Killer whale

Library of Congress Cataloging-in-Publication Data

Behrens, June.
  Whales of the world.

  Summary: Describes the behavior, habitats, and
individual species of whales and dolphins, including
the bottlenose dolphin, humpback whale, and right
whale.
  1. Whales—Juvenile literature. 2. Dolphins—
Juvenile literature. [1. Whales. 2. Dolphins]
I. Title.
QL737.C4B54 1987   599.5   87-8046
ISBN 0-516-08877-7

Childrens Press, Chicago.
Copyright ©1987 by Regensteiner Publishing Enterprises, Inc.
All rights reserved. Published simultaneously in Canada.
Printed in the United States of America.
    4 5 6 7 8 9 10 R 96 95 94 93 92 91 90

The author wishes to acknowledge with thanks the assistance of the following people in the preparation of this manuscript:

John Olguin, Cabrillo Marine Museum
Bill Samaras, American Cetacean Society

Dedication: Al and Trish Artuso

Dolphins can be trained to do tricks.

Humpback whale cow with her calf

Of all the creatures on this earth, whales are the largest. They are the most powerful.

Whales live in all the oceans of the world, yet they are not fish. They are warm-blooded animals with a backbone. Like all mammals,

4

baby whales drink their mother's milk.
Whales breathe air and are covered with
skin.

Scientists call whales cetaceans. Cetaceans
are large sea mammals that live in water.
The great whales and their smaller relatives,
dolphins and porpoises, are cetaceans.

Right whale with her calf

Whales range in size from the four-foot porpoise up to the 100-foot blue whale. The blue whale is one-third the length of a football field.

Most whales like to be with one another. They are social animals and they travel in groups called schools or pods. Whales must come to the surface of the water to breathe through their nostrils, which are called

Common dolphin

Blue whale with vapor spout

blowholes. The blowhole is on the top of the whale's head. Air passes in and out of the whale's lungs through its blowhole.

When whales breathe the air out, it becomes a vapor spout. The vapor spout is a mixture of air, gases and condensed water from the whale's breath. This vapor spout looks like a fountain. It might go fifteen feet in the air!

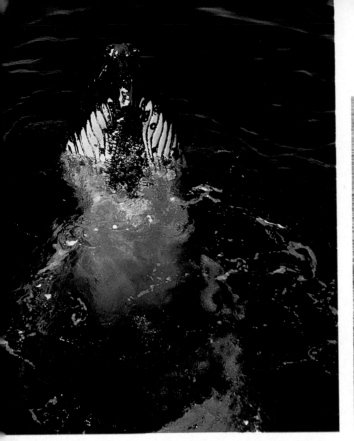

Humpback whale leaping out of the water (left) and swimming on its back (right) with its flippers in the air

The blowhole is tightly closed when the whale dives below the surface of the water. Some whales can hold their breath for over an hour before they come up for air.

Most whales and dolphins swim near the surface of the water. Others, like the sperm whales, are deep-sea divers. They dive for deep-water squid.

Whales have flippers. The flippers are used as paddles. They help balance and steer the whale in the water. The two parts of the whale's tail are called flukes. The flukes move up and down. They push the whale through the water.

Tail flukes of a humpback whale

Killer whale with calf

Mother whales are called cows, and their young are called calves. After the calf is born, the cow pushes it to the surface of the water. The baby gets its first breath of air.

Calves can swim as soon as they are born. The newly born calf of one blue whale measured over 24 feet long!

Some whales have teeth. Others do not.
Whales with teeth are called toothed whales.
Those without teeth are called baleen
whales.

The baleen, or whalebone, whale has
blades of whalebone that hang down from

Teeth of a killer whale (left) and close-up of baleen (right) in the
mouth of a sei whale.

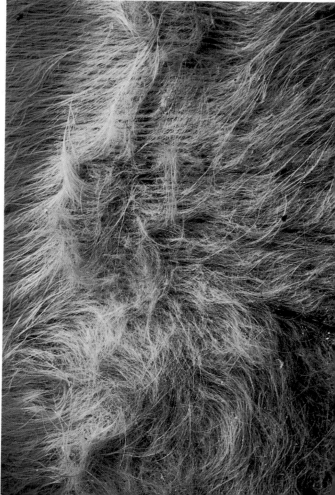

The humpback feeds with its mouth open, trapping small sea creatures in its baleen.

the roof of its mouth. The blades act as a giant strainer, or sieve. The baleen whale swims with its mouth open, trapping small sea creatures in its whalebone plates. Then the whale closes its mouth. It uses its tongue to scrape food off the sieve and swallow it.

Baleen whales have two blowholes. Although they are the largest members of the whale family, they eat some of the smallest plants and animals in the sea. Baleen whales include the Atlantic and Pacific right whale, the finback, the sei, the minke, and the humpback whales. The blue and the Pacific gray whales are also baleen whales.

Close-up of a humpback whale's two blowholes

All other whales belong to the toothed whale group. There are many more toothed whales, and they are smaller than the baleen whales. Toothed whales have piercing teeth and large throats. They can swallow chunks of seafood and whole fish. Killer whales eat seals and birds and sometimes other whales.

The killer whale is a toothed whale.

Beluga whale swimming in Canada's Churchill River

Toothed whales have one blowhole. Sperm whales, porpoises, and dolphins belong to this group. The white whale, the beaked whale, the bottlenose whale, and the narwhal are also toothed whales.

Where do whales live?

Whales live in all oceans and some freshwater rivers. They live where they can find a food supply. Some migrate, or move, from one place to another when the seasons change.

Blue Whales are the largest animals known. They get their name from their dark-blue coloring. Blues live in polar seas and deep-ocean waters. These baleen whales feed on tiny sea life called krill. The stomach of a blue whale can hold more than two tons of food. Blue whales have measured over 100 feet in length. One giant weighed nearly 200 tons—almost 400,000 pounds!

The blue whale is a powerful swimmer.

Blue whales migrate. They swim to warmer waters to mate and give birth to their young.

The blues leave their polar feeding grounds and move to warmer waters to mate. In the warmer seas the females give birth to their young. The young drink their mother's milk and almost double their weight each week. With the change of seasons, the blues return with their calves to the polar feeding grounds.

In the past, whalers killed blue whales by the thousands. Finally, there were very few left. People feared that they would become extinct, or disappear forever. Today there are laws to protect them.

Finback whale

 Finback Whales are fast swimmers and the
second largest of the great whales. They are
at home in the oceans of the world. They
move from cooler to warmer climates.
Finbacks have a large dorsal fin on their
backs. Their upper bodies are dark and the
undersides are white.

 Sperm Whales are found in tropical waters
and open oceans. They are the largest of the
toothed whales. They often swim in waters
off North America and sometimes they move

to the polar seas. Sperm whales have a head about one-third the length of their bodies. They are deep-sea divers. They go deep down into the ocean to find the giant squid they like to eat.

Sperm whales have a huge square snout. It contains almost a ton of oil. The early whalers hunted for sperm whales. These whales were made famous by a book called *Moby Dick*.

The sperm whale has a square snout.

Right Whales were named by early whalers who thought they were the right whales to hunt. They are very slow-moving and easy to kill. They float when they are dead. Whalers brought home valuable oil and whalebone from their catch of right whales.

Greenland right whales, or bowhead whales, are found in Arctic waters. These baleen whales have a huge curved upper jaw. They can weigh up to 100 tons.

Bowhead whale swimming with beluga whales

Right whale swimming with its mouth partly open

Biscayan, or black whales, are members of the right whale family. They live in warmer waters. These whales were hunted off the Spanish coast almost 1000 years ago.

Pygmy right whales might be found in New Zealand, South American, or South African waters. They like the foods found in the southern oceans. These twenty-foot whales are the smallest of the right whale family.

Humpback whale surfacing in Hawaii

Humpback Whales live in polar waters in the summer where they feed. They move to warmer climates near the equator in the winter. Here they give birth to their calves. Whale watchers in Hawaii enjoy the antics of humpbacks during this season.

Humpbacks have long flippers. They leap into the air and round, or hump, their backs as they dive. Humpbacks "spy-hop," or appear to stand with their heads above the water. They wave their enormous flippers. They are curious and often swim near boats.

Whale watching off the coast of New England

Gray whale in British Columbia

Pacific Gray Whales are found in the Pacific Ocean along the western coast of the United States. Each year they travel, or migrate, over 10,000 miles. Grays make the round trip from Alaskan waters to the lagoons in Mexico to mate and have their young.

Grays are covered with white blotchy scars and barnacles. They have a gray coloring and are easily seen from shore. People on the Pacific coast enjoy watching the yearly winter migration of the gray whales.

Whale watchers photograph a migrating gray whale.

Sei Whales live in the open ocean. They like the food in the coldest waters of the oceans. Sei whales are the smaller giants, seldom growing over 60 feet long. Their slender bodies are fast moving and powerful.

Head of a sei whale

Bryde's whale eats krill, too.

Bryde's Whales like warm water and live in tropical seas. They are found in waters near the West Indies and southern and western Africa. They are about the size of sei whales. Bryde's whales eat fish, including herring and mackerel.

Northern bottlenose whale

Bottlenose Whales belong to the beaked whale family. They have beaks with only one or two pairs of teeth. Northern bottlenose whales have a rounded forehead. They live in deep oceans in the North Atlantic. Southern bottlenose whales are found in waters off Australia and Argentina.

Male Narwhal, or *Unicorn Whales*, make their year-round home in Arctic waters. The left tooth in their upper jaw grows into a tusk. This tusk sometimes grows to ten feet!

The male narwhal (left) grows a single tusk. Narwhals (right) live in Arctic waters.

Beluga whale (left) performs tricks at an aquarium. School of beluga whales (right)

Beluga, or *White Whales*, as adults are pure white. They live in Arctic waters, but have sometimes traveled as far south as New England. Beluga whales swim in schools of over a hundred.

Orca, or *Killer Whales*, have shiny black and white bodies with a six-foot fin on their back. These meat-eaters are found mostly in polar seas. Killer whales travel in schools of thirty to forty. They attack and eat birds and seals, dolphins and whales. Killer whales have been known to herd fish. A group will circle a school of fish. One whale will eat while the others keep the fish penned in.

Killer whales swim and hunt together.

Pilot whale leaps out of the water.

Pilot Whales, or *Blackfish*, are found in the Pacific, Atlantic, and Indian oceans. They follow their leaders from warm to cold waters. Pilot whales travel in large schools of several hundred. Sometimes whales swim ashore and become stranded on beaches. No one knows why.

Dolphins are smaller members of the Cetacean or whale family. Most have a snout like a beak, one blowhole, and teeth. The more than thirty species, or kinds, of dolphins live in all the oceans of the world.

Bottlenose Dolphins are the best known of the dolphin family. Most are found in the Atlantic and the northern and southern Pacific oceans. These dolphins are very intelligent. They can be taught to bring and carry objects. They like the company of humans. Flipper, of TV fame, was a bottlenose dolphin.

Atlantic bottlenose dolphin

Common Dolphins are found in the Mediterranean Sea and in most oceans. They are about eight feet long and have many teeth in both jaws.

River Dolphins swim in freshwater rivers. They live in the Amazon River in South America, the Ganges River in India, and the Yangtze River in China. River dolphins have long, beaked snouts and as many as 200 sharp teeth.

Playful common dolphins (left) and the Ganges River dolphin (above)

Close-up of the teeth and snout of an Atlantic Harbor porpoise

Porpoises are smaller than dolphins. They are fatter and have a rounded snout. Porpoises live in coastal waters and eat the available fish. There are only six species of porpoises.

Whale Migration

Many whales migrate. This means they move from one place to another in the oceans of the world. Whales travel from season to season. Their feeding grounds may be in the colder seas. When it is the season to mate and have their young, they move to warmer waters.

Migrating whales include the right, the humpback, the blue, and the gray whales.

Some whales do not migrate. Belugas, narwhals, and bowheads seem to stay in their cold Arctic waters.

One of the best-known whale migrations is that of the Pacific gray whales. From December to February they swim south along the Pacific Coast.

Humpback whale migrating to warmer waters

Gray whale cow traveling with her calf

The grays travel in small groups of three or more. In warm Mexican lagoons, they mate and have their calves. In March and April the grays make their return trip up the Pacific coast. When the calves and mothers swim back from their feeding grounds in the Arctic, they can be seen from shore.

Whales Talk and Sing

Members of the whale family make many different sounds. There are low singers and high-pitched whistlers. Whales make feeding sounds and mating sounds. They talk to each other in clicks and groans.

Their whistles and squeaks seem to have special meanings. They use sound signals to find their way. Cries of a whale in distress have brought others from miles away.

Scientist records whale sounds.

Beluga whales

Dolphins can be taught to imitate human sounds. Belugas are called sea canaries. Their whistles and squeals are heard above the water of their Arctic homes. Gray whales talk in grunts, cracking sounds, and whistles.

The humpback whale sings. Sounds from high-pitched screams to low throbs may continue for ten to fifteen minutes. They are repeated over and over. Songs of the humpback whales have been recorded. They have been known to sing six different songs.

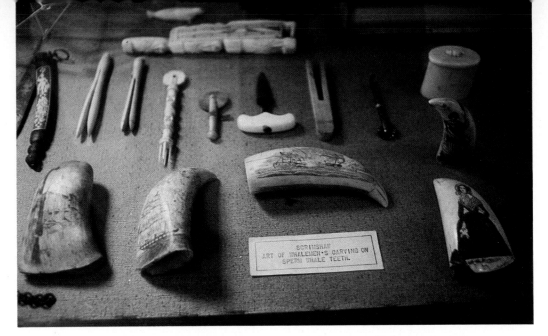

Scrimshaw, carvings made on whalebone or whale ivory, are displayed at the Whaling Museum in Mystic, Connecticut.

Friends and Helpers

From earliest times, stories have been told about the whale family. Ancient Greeks and Romans made pictures of dolphins on their coins and vases. They told picture stories on their walls of friendships between children and dolphins.

Dolphins have been called friends of man. They like to race with ships. They have saved the lives of drowning people. A

Dolphins are friendly and smart.

bottlenose dolphin made friends with the children playing in Hokianga Harbor in New Zealand. It swam and played with the bathers often. The children called their new friend "Opo."

Dolphins have helped stranded whales find their way back to the open sea. Recently, when a herd of pilot whales became grounded on a New Zealand beach, the townspeople came out to help. They managed to turn the whales around. A nearby school of dolphins swam in and began to move around among the whales. They guided the stranded animals out to sea and safety.

Dead finback whale

Killer whales perform at Sea World in San Diego.

How Smart are Whales?

Scientists say that whales are very intelligent. Smaller members of the whale family can be trained, and they learn quickly. They have been taught to do amazing tricks for a reward of fish and attention. Many trainers believe that dolphins can think.

This porpoise was trained to handle underwater equipment.

The U.S. Navy has trained small whales to do secret work. Dolphins and porpoises have learned to protect men against sharks and to carry tools to working divers. Once, an aquanaut diver lost his grip on a lifeline and could not find his way back. A trained porpoise named Tuffy found the aquanaut and carried a lifeline to him.

Members of the whale family are mammals, just as humans are mammals. Humans are the guardians of the whale population. Overhunting by whalers has made the blues, finbacks, and humpbacks endangered species. Worldwide laws must be enforced to keep whales safe in the oceans of the world.

Many people join "Save the whale" groups to protect these harmless mammals from hunters.

BALEEN WHALES

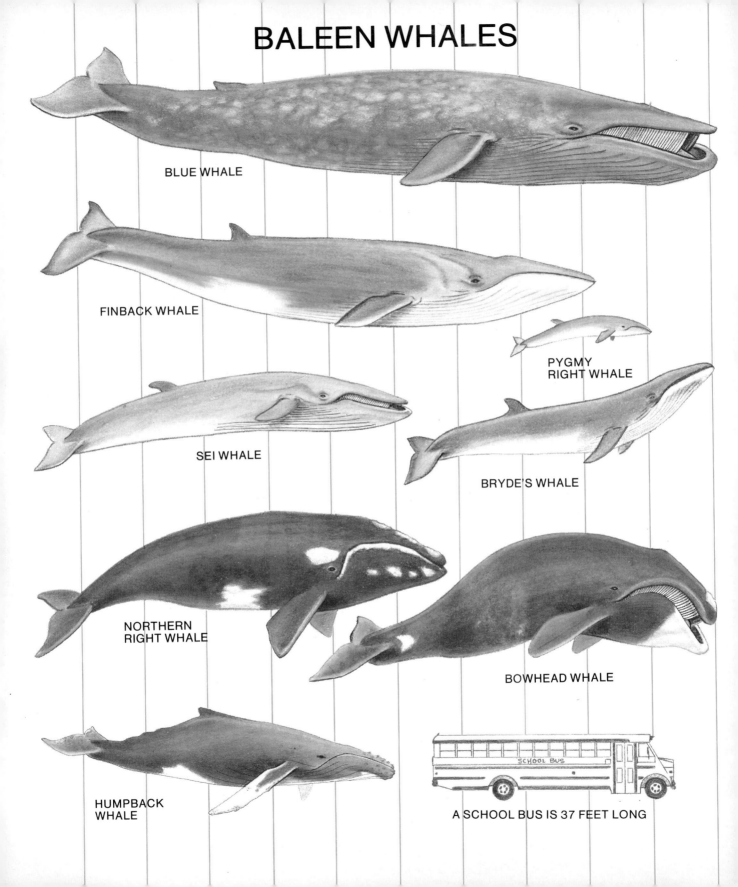

BLUE WHALE

FINBACK WHALE

PYGMY RIGHT WHALE

SEI WHALE

BRYDE'S WHALE

NORTHERN RIGHT WHALE

BOWHEAD WHALE

HUMPBACK WHALE

SCHOOL BUS

A SCHOOL BUS IS 37 FEET LONG

BALEEN WHALES

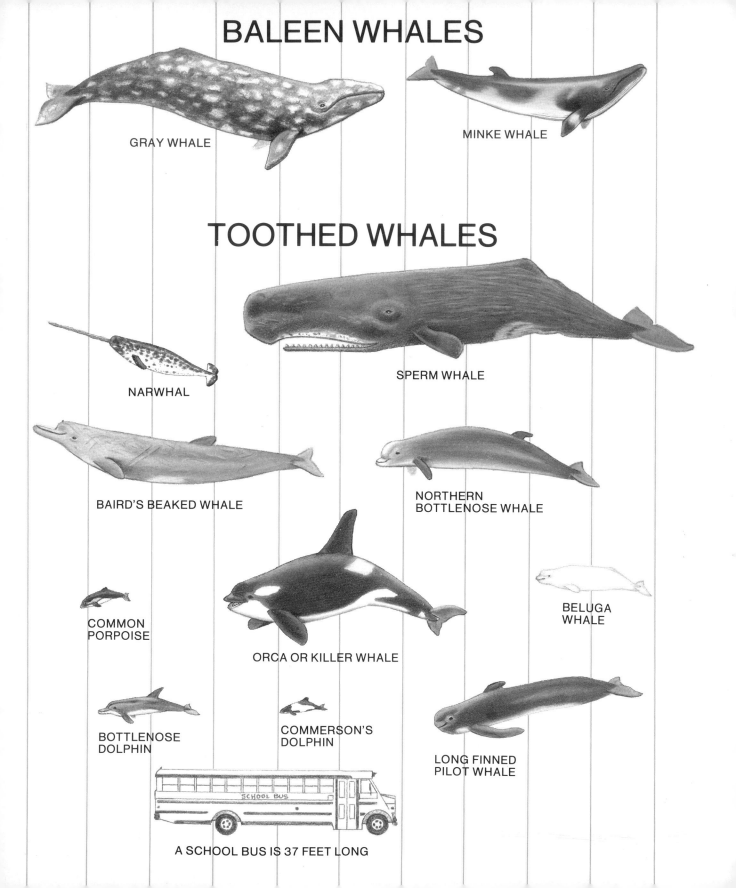

GRAY WHALE

MINKE WHALE

TOOTHED WHALES

NARWHAL

SPERM WHALE

BAIRD'S BEAKED WHALE

NORTHERN
BOTTLENOSE WHALE

COMMON
PORPOISE

ORCA OR KILLER WHALE

BELUGA
WHALE

BOTTLENOSE
DOLPHIN

COMMERSON'S
DOLPHIN

LONG FINNED
PILOT WHALE

SCHOOL BUS

A SCHOOL BUS IS 37 FEET LONG

Dolphin

ABOUT THE AUTHOR

For the past 25 years June Behrens has been writing for children. Her many years as an educator have made her sensitive to the interests and needs of young readers. Mrs. Behrens has written over 60 books, touching on a wide range of subjects in both fiction and nonfiction. June Behrens received her academic education from the University of California at Santa Barbara, where she was honored as Distinguished Alumni of the Year for her contributions to the field of education. She has a Master's degree from the University of Southern California. Mrs. Behrens is listed in *Who's Who of American Women*. She lives with her husband in Rancho Palos Verdes, near Los Angeles.